PROCEEDINGS

AT

THE DEDICATION

OF

THE CITY HALL,

SEPTEMBER 18, 1865.

BOSTON:
LISHED BY ORDER OF THE CITY COUNCIL.
1865.

CITY OF BOSTON.

In Common Council, Sept. 21, 1865.

ORDERED: That His Honor the Mayor be requested to furnish a copy of the beautiful and appropriate Address, delivered by him at the Dedication of the City Hall on Monday last, and that the same be published in connection with the other commemorative services of that occasion.

Passed: Sent up for concurrence.

WM. B. FOWLE, *President.*

In Board of Aldermen, Sept. 25, 1865.

Concurred:

G. W. MESSINGER, *Chairman.*

A true copy.

Attest: H. T. ROCKWELL,

City Clerk, pro tempore.

DEDICATION

OF

THE CITY HALL.

On Monday, September 18,* 1865, at 12 o'clock, M. a joint convention of both branches of the City Council was held in the Council Chamber, at the new City Hall, for the purpose of dedicating the building to the use of the City Government of Boston. Upon taking the chair, His Honor the Mayor stated the object of the meeting, and called upon Alderman Daniel Davies, the Chairman of the Committee on Public Buildings, who had charge of the work, to proceed in the discharge of his official duty.

Alderman Davies then came forward and made the following remarks: —

MR. MAYOR: It becomes my duty, as Chairman of the Committee on Public Buildings, to surrender to you, the chief executive officer of this city, this building, which has been erected by the direction of the City Council for the purposes of a City Hall.

* The seventeenth of September, the anniversary of the foundation of Boston, occurred on Sunday, and the services were postponed, therefore, until the next day.

On the first day of July, 1862, the orders were received by the Committee directing them to erect suitable buildings for a City Hall. During the fall and winter of 1862 the contracts were made for the excavation, the stone work, masonry, and carpentry. A portion of the foundation being ready on the 22d day of December, the corner-stone was laid, which finished the work for that year. Early the next spring the work was recommenced, and it has been constantly prosecuted to the present time. As a full description, with plans of the building and grounds, the names of the contractors, and portions of work performed by each, and the expense of the work, will soon be printed in detail, it is unnecessary to give them at this time.

Although considerable work yet remains to be done, it was thought best by the Committee that the building should be formally dedicated on this day, — the anniversary of the foundation of the town of Boston.

And now, Mr. Mayor, under the direction and in behalf of the Committee on Public Buildings, I surrender to your charge this building, and deliver to you this key, which controls its entrance.

To these remarks the Mayor responded as follows :—

Mr. Chairman: As the representative of the Executive Government of Boston, it is my duty, as well as my privilege, to receive from your hands this key, as a formal delivery of this beautiful edifice. The peculiar felicity of the Committee on Public Buildings is, that their work appears in a tangible form ; it is not placed upon file, or bound up with the City Documents, but appears in our public streets, and, while ministering to the wants of the people, gratifies the taste and embellishes and ornaments the city. The degree of opulence and wealth which a community has attained is indicated by the character of its public buildings ; and although the useful purposes to which they are devoted are of more vital consequence than their mere form, yet the harmonious combination of the practical with the beautiful carries with it a higher illustration of the culture and refinement of the people. It has been your privilege, together with that of your associates, in addition to the usual work committed to your charge, — such as the building of public stables and engine houses, police stations, hospitals, and school-houses, — to be called upon to superintend the erection of this crowning glory of municipal architecture,—an edifice wisely adapted to the official and business purposes of the government, and also an expressive and imposing structure, typifying by its costly and elaborate embellishments the dignity and relative rank of our city. It is a subject of just pride to our citizens that within a few years there has been a marked change in the outward appearance and style of all classes of our buildings. The stranger, who from time to time visits our metropolis, must be impressed with the architectural progress which has been made in the character of our private dwellings, as well as those devoted to science and art and to the worship of Almighty God.

While public-spirited individuals have united their means for the erection of many elegant structures appropriated to the institutions which bless our people, the city itself, through its municipal authorities, has not been negligent of its duty in this respect.

Whatever difference of opinion may have existed as to the expediency of erecting a new City Hall at a time when the dark cloud of civil war was hanging over the country, yet its completion is celebrated when the bright beams of peace are cheering the hearts of the people. As the work on the magnificent Capitol at Washington, in which the National Council holds its session, still resolutely went on during the dark period, so we, with an unfaltering faith in the success of the country's cause, abated not one jot or tittle in our original design. The inflation of the currency and other circumstances may have swelled the figures on our Treasurer's books; but we believe we have presented to our constituents a building worth all it has cost.

For the patient assiduity and skilful manner in which you, Mr. Chairman, and your associates of the

Committee, have discharged the special duties incumbent on your official position, I have no doubt you will receive the thanks of our citizens. This building will long remain a memorial of your devotion to the public service, and a monument to the taste of the architects who designed, and the faithful Boston mechanics who have been engaged in its erection.

As the organ of the City Government I cheerfully receive it from your hands, with sincere congratulations on the near approach of the consummation of your labors in its behalf.

Rev. Chandler Robbins, D. D., pastor of the Second Church, offered the following prayer: —

Almighty and most merciful God, our Father which art in heaven, hallowed be Thy name! We would come together for the first time into these goodly halls with devout acknowledgments of Thy glory and Thy goodness, and of our dependence and obligations.

We adore Thee as the Architect and Owner of the heavens, and the earth, and all things which they contain. Remembering that "except the Lord build the house, they labor in vain that build it," we would thank Thee that Thy Providence has worked together with those whose skill and strength have reared this edifice; that while stone has been laid upon stone and beam upon beam, no hostile power has marred the work or destroyed the workmen. We thank Thee that by Thy favor it stands complete, and that the various officers of our municipal government are permitted, under such auspicious circumstances, to take possession of its ample and commodious apartments and to dedicate them to their public uses. May they come into its unpolluted walls with clean hands and pure hearts, with new purposes of fidelity, and new interest in all that concerns the welfare of our city and its inhabitants.

We thank Thee for all the historic recollections, both of civic and national interest, which this occasion revives. We thank Thee that Thou didst lead our pilgrim ancestors across the ocean, and guard and guide them, while with toils and prayers they laid the foundation of this city, and of a new empire in the west. We thank Thee for their faith and their piety, their patience and their trust, their love of liberty and respect for law, their fidelity to conscience, their political wisdom and their practical energy, for all those qualities which fitted them for the successful performance of the work which Thy Providence laid upon them, and the fruits of which we are this day enjoying. We thank Thee for all and each of those wise and faithful men, in the long line of their successors, who, in their respective generations, have contributed in any way to promote the true prosperity and establish the fair fame of Boston.

The whole history of our city is one continued record of Thy favors. May we not be ungrateful. May we not be unworthy of such a past. May we not be forgetful of the hand that has built us up and the mercy that has blessed us. Let us emulate the virtues and public spirit of our fathers, and not through pride and impiety fall away from honoring and serving our fathers' God.

As our thoughts revert on this anniversary to the adoption of that Constitution which formed the basis of our national union, we would with one accord offer our thanksgivings and supplications in behalf of our country. We would remember with gratitude how Thou didst watch over the infant Republic, and protect it from foreign enemies; how Thou didst enlarge its borders and increase its greatness; how Thou didst nourish and defend it till it took its place among the leading nations of the earth; and when in these latter years intestine discord threatened its destruction, how Thy Right Hand and Thine Arm saved and delivered us. We thank Thee, O gracious Lord, that Thou hast brought us out of all the horrors and miseries of a fratricidal war, and art cheering and comforting us with the blessings of reviving peace. O grant, we beseech Thee, that it may be a righteous and permanent peace. As we lay aside the weapons of warfare, dispose and help us to put away from us forever those lusts and iniquities which were the cause of the war, and which would be a perpetual source of future discord and calamity. Taught by the bitter discipline through which we have passed, may we become a wise, just, and Christian people.

Bless, we entreat Thee, the President of the United States. Enlighten his mind, that he may discern what is for the true interest of the Republic. Enlarge and purify his heart, that he may be both liberal and just. Strengthen his hands, that he may firmly execute the laws and vigorously carry into effect wise and equitable measures for the reconciliation and reconstruction of our disordered nation. Endue the members of his Cabinet, and all who are connected with the administration of the National Government with understanding and virtue. Discarding selfish ambition and party prejudice, may they work together faithfully and successfully, with one mind, and in the fear of God, for their country's good.

And now, O God, we would humbly and fervently commend to Thy continued protection and favor our beloved city; its Chief Magistrate, and all the members of its government, and all who are associated with its service; its institutions of learning, science, charity, justice, and religion; the interests of its trade, commerce and industry, and all the instruments and elements of its prosperity. Save it from those things which divide, corrupt, and disgrace a people; save it from luxury, intemperance, faction, infidelity, and every form of vice and ungodliness. May it be the home of order, concord, health, intelligence, and humanity; of all the virtues which ennoble, the arts which adorn and refine, and the Christian faith and piety which exalt a city.

Let this edifice, dedicated and set apart to municipal services and duties, be a centre of good and salutary influences. Here may men of integrity, discretion, and practical ability, consult harmoniously, legislate wisely, and act impartially, for the public good. May it stand for many years a tower of defence as well as an ornament. As it shall become venerable from age, may it become more and more venerable from association with the worthy names and faithful services of those who shall have occupied it. And, long after its walls shall have crumbled, may the spot on which it stands be surrounded by the abodes of a prosperous and Christian people.

O, God, in Thy great mercy, accept these our thanksgivings and prayers, forgive and cleanse us from our sins, and help us to live to Thy glory. May all the kingdoms and inhabitants of the world be blessed with the knowledge of Thy truth and the experience of Thy saving health. Give to Thy dear son Jesus Christ, our Lord, the sceptre of the nations, that he may reign over them in righteousness and peace. In him may our prayers be heard, our offerings be accepted and our works blessed, and through him we will render unto Thee all praise and glory forever. Amen.

The Mayor then delivered the following address: —

ADDRESS.

ADDRESS

OF THE MAYOR,

FREDERIC W. LINCOLN, JR.

Gentlemen of the City Council, and Fellow Citizens: We are assembled on an occasion which will hereafter mark an important era in the municipal history of Boston. We have met this day to dedicate, with appropriate ceremonies, a new building to be devoted to the local administration of the affairs of this city. On this two hundred and thirty-fifth anniversary of its civic birth, our minds are naturally and fondly carried back through the stirring events of these many years. The long procession of noble men, who have given it a name and character, again pass on the stage before us. We watch with intense interest the movements of the fathers of the town, who, self-exiled from the land of their birth and the sepulchres of their ancestors, landed upon these shores, and, building a home for themselves and their little ones, laid the foundations of a city which should be known and honored through many generations. We would bow in reverence to the motives which led them to form this infant settlement. They were not mere adventurers, — the cast-off mendicants from the Old World; many of them were men of culture and education; some with a fair share of worldly goods, all of an incorruptible integrity; yet they left the conveniences and comforts of their native land to found, upon the barren strand of a New World, a state where the privileges of civil and religious liberty, of which they had been deprived by arbitrary power, might be enjoyed by themselves and their posterity. The success which crowned their efforts is illustrated in every page of our annals, and is to be seen in our present condition and prosperity. Boston, the capital of Massachusetts Bay, through all its colonial and provincial existence, affords one of the best examples of the steady development and progress of civil freedom, culminating in the revolutionary era, when the sister colonies, espousing her cause, united in the Declaration of Independence, thus establishing the Republic of the United States, and introducing a new people into the family of nations.

Our local history commences with September seventh, old style, or September seventeenth, new style, 1630, when the Court of Assistants of Massachusetts Bay, then sitting at Charlestown, acting under a charter granted by Charles the First, ordered that this peninsula, which had heretofore been called Shawmut and Trimountain, should take the name of Boston. Such were the peculiar associations connected with Boston in England, that the leaders in the enterprise had resolved, previous to embarking from their homes, that the chief town should be called by this name. Boston had been famous in the annals of the persecuted Puritans; a large portion of the company belonged to that city and the county of Lincoln, in which it is situated; and it is said that the name was also considered as a compliment to the Rev. John Cotton, a distinguished clergyman of that place, who united his fame and fortune with them, and afterwards became the pastor of the First Church in the new settlement.

It was thus early decided, on account of its natural advantages, to be the capital of the colony. There were other places which had been settled previously, which had a claim to the distinction, such as Salem, Dorchester, Charlestown, and Cambridge, but its rapid growth and prosperity soon justified the wisdom of the selection. It was designed for a commercial town, was limited in extent, and was sometimes designated "Blackstone's Neck," after the first settler. Its greatest wants were wood and meadow land, so that those of the people "who lived upon their cattle" took farms in the adjoining country, which were granted to them for the purpose. It was feared by many that it would be no place for continued habitation, for want of a staple commodity; but, as early as 1647, her interests had become diversified; she not only raised from the earth and the sea enough for all her inhabitants, but had a large commerce with Virginia, Barbadoes, and the Summer Islands; with France, Spain, Portugal, and Holland, and even with England.

Johnson says, in speaking of the colony of Massachusetts Bay, that "the maritime towns began to increase roundly, especially Boston, the which of a poor country village in twice seven years it became like unto a small city, and is in election to be Mayor Town suddenly, chiefly increased by trade by sea." He also says, at an earlier date, that "it is the centre town and the metropolis of this wilderness work, and its continual enlargement presages some sumptuous city."

There is no clear account of the commencement of our municipal government. The records in the possession of our City Clerk do not give any light on the subject. The affairs of the colony and the town were so connected, as it was the seat of government, that probably at first the Governor and Assistants, the majority being inhabitants of the town, exercised all the powers that were necessary. Sometimes there appear upon the records "Overseers of the Town's Concerns," or "persons chosen for the occasion of the town." But in 1645 a regular Board of Selectmen was chosen, John

Winthrop, that year acting as Deputy Governor of the Colony, being Chairman, and James Penn, one of their number, Recorder and Treasurer. As the town increased in population and wealth, frequent attempts were made by a portion of the inhabitants to secure for it the name and privileges of a city. As early as 1651 the subject was agitated; again in 1708, in 1762, in 1784, in 1815, and finally with success in 1822. The whole number of votes cast was four thousand eight hundred and eleven; the number in favor of the City Government was two thousand eight hundred and five; the number against the project was two thousand and six. A charter was obtained from the Legislature, which received the signature of Governor Brooks, February 23, 1822, and was accepted by the people on the following fourth of March. The new government was organized at Faneuil Hall on the first of May, the Chairman of the Selectmen, Eliphalet Williams, in an appropriate speech, transferring the powers of the old town organization to the Mayor, John Phillips, who delivered an inaugural address, — the oath of office being administered by Chief Justice Parker, and a prayer offered by the Rev. Dr. Baldwin, the senior clergyman of the town.

No single thing affords a better illustration of the character of the people of Boston than their long continued love for a democratic form of municipal organization. It was only when the population became so large that their interests suffered materially by the old customs, that they would consent to delegate the powers of the local government to a limited number of their town fellow-citizens. A watchful and jealous scrutiny of the conduct of their official servants is still a marked characteristic of Boston, and woe will befall our city when the great body of her citizens cease to take an interest in her public affairs.

You will not expect me, gentlemen, on an occasion like the present, to deliver an historical discourse upon so inspiring a theme as the annals of Boston, tempting though it be. I have alluded to the commencement of our town, because the associations connected with this anniversary required it, and in order that we may be reminded of the days of small things, and of the great contrast between the distant past, and the present of which we form a part. To the student of history, I verily believe there is no more interesting study to be found, than the record of the events which have made Boston what she is to-day. He will find that she has had a healthy and well-developed progress in everything which promotes the welfare of civilized man, — the cause of religion and morals, education and science, commerce and industry, good order and social happiness. While the machinery of town government, based upon the example of the mother country, was followed so far as it suited her condition, yet better methods and additional institutions were organized, more wisely adapted to the character and prospective wants of the people.

The stirring events which made her name famous in the revolutionary era has somewhat overshadowed her earlier history; but I contend her career has been brilliant from the first; and her intrepid stand against the encroachments of arbitrary power at that time, was but the natural consequence of that education and discipline which her people had been receiving for a century and a half in the defence of their colonial and provincial rights. There is not a more pregnant page in the records of the progress of mankind towards civil liberty than the part which our town took in that long struggle, in which she was finally defeated, when the original charter of Massachusetts Bay was taken from the colony, and it became a province of the King. Then commenced a new era in her history, apparently dark, but gradually lighting up as she successively combated and defied the several British governors, who, representing the prerogatives of the Crown, claimed her slavish allegiance, until she had the happiness of seeing the last of the loyal line forced to take his departure from the town, and sail down the waters of our beautiful bay with his mercenary troops, never more to return. The events of the revolutionary period are as familiar to us as "household words." As

Boston was the theatre where its great principles were earliest discussed and promulgated, so was its vicinity the scene of some of its most important engagements when an appeal was made to arms. The long struggle on other fields, and in different parts of the country, she sustained with men and means in a cheerful spirit; and when peace came, her people, and especially her mechanics, spoke with a resolution which could not be resisted, in behalf of the adoption of the Federal Constitution, which was the glorious consummation of the patriot's prayers and the bright herald of the nation's prosperity. At the advent of the new government under Washington, the country, saved by the valor of her sons, and the Union, consolidated by the provisions of this immortal instrument, Boston again started on her onward course. Her representatives took a leading part in the National Councils, while her citizens at home embarked in new enterprises for the development of the commercial and industrial resources of the country. The keels of her merchant ships vexed the seas of every continent. Her capitalists made the streams of New England, as they descended to the ocean, work their passage as manufactories were planted on their murmuring courses. Her mechanics and artisans, invigorated by the new motives to labor which independence had secured, added new wealth to the community; and her professional men of every class gave a fresh lustre to science, and dedicated their learning to the advancement and elevation of mankind. In the history of the last half century, she has been in unison with the rapid progress and marvellous success of our common country. Her wealth and population have increased with a healthy and steady growth. Often reproached as the representative of ideas in advance of the public sentiment of the whole Union, she to-day is honored as never before for her unflinching adherence to principle, and the Republic itself will not part with her fame or the renown of her great men so long as it holds a place in the front rank of the constitutional governments of the world.

I must confess to you that, in the preparation for this occasion, among the multitude of subjects, I have found it difficult to so order my thoughts as to select the appropriate topics for consideration. The primary cause which led our ancestors to this place was religion ; and it would be an interesting field of survey to trace the progress of religious thought and theological inquiry, — to see how, with the advance of years, the tenets of the older sects were liberalized and new churches planted and prospered, so that now, living in harmony, we have the representatives of all the denominations into which the Christian world is divided. Education was the stone upon which our fathers laid the foundation of their superstructure ;

and this interest has been so prominent through our history, that the modern friends of free schools have sometimes considered it our special token of regard, and other communities have gladly followed in the intellectual paths which we have marked out for ourselves. I believe it is generally acknowledged, that there is no large city in the world where the people of every class are so well versed in the common rudiments of knowledge; and certainly there is none in comparison with the population where there are so many institutions devoted to the higher branches of scientific investigation, and to the encouragement of elegant literature and the fine arts. Institutions for charitable and philanthropic purposes have always been fostered, keeping pace with human wants and needs, so that hardly an "ill which flesh is heir to" is left neglected in the circle of our ministering agencies.

The glorious success of our national arms in crushing the late Rebellion and extirpating that foul blot on the nation's character, which has so long been our reproach, will have an important effect on our commercial and industrial relations. Channels of business heretofore obstructed, or undeveloped, will soon open to the spirit of adventure or enterprise. Holding fast on those methods and objects of traffic which have been a source of her worldly success, Boston is destined to expand still more in this direction; and that prosperity which is based upon a mutual interchange of the commodities of the earth with the handicraft of man, can be anticipated for our city with the liveliest feelings of hope and cheer. A modern teacher of political economy has a maxim, that, "to increase the wealth of a people, you add to their power to bless the world." We, therefore, may rejoice from the highest motives, at all the signs of an affluent city which appear, if we constantly bear in mind that our duties correspond with the privileges we enjoy.

Another class of subjects pertinent to the occasion, if time would permit, would be a consideration of the various interests directly connected with the special prerogatives and duties of a municipal government. The topographical changes which have taken place in the town since its settlement, have been as marked as any in its history. Commencing on a peninsula of about seven hundred acres, with its additional territory, mostly reclaimed from the sea, it is now not far from sixteen hundred acres; while East Boston and South Boston, now single wards, have each an extent of surface suitable for habitations and business purposes larger than the original town. Some of the prominent hills in the City proper have been levelled, and its creeks have been filled up. Many of its ancient streets, following the line of the shore, or creeping at the base of its original heights, or suiting themselves to the diversities of the surface of the soil, have been straightened and widened ; and this is a work which must go on, to meet the new exigencies of a teeming and thriving population, — a prolific source of official business, and involving a large expenditure of the public money. Our harbor, naturally one of the most magnificent in the world, whose spacious and convenient waters were the very cause of the location of the town, has, through the ravages of the sea, been seriously impaired, and deserves the most careful management, especially in those schemes for the city's enlargement, which an increasing commerce may require. When we consider the millions of people who are in the future to inhabit this continent, and are to form this energetic and busy nation, and recollect that the good harbors on the Atlantic coast, which connect us with the old world, can be counted on one's fingers, while this geographical fact presages that Boston will always hold an important commercial position, yet it gives a new significance to this interest so vital to its prosperity.

The sanitary condition of our city, always a matter of concern with our ancestors, as is seen in their early appointment of a board of health, becomes more and more a subject of municipal care as population increases. The liberal supply and proper distribution of water, the fire department, which protects our dwellings and warehouses from the devouring element, the police, who shield us from the designs and acts of wicked men, the institutions where the vicious are incarcerated, or the unfortunate or the insane find their homes, the finances of the city, the construction of sewers, the paving and lighting of streets, the markets, cemeteries, hospitals, public library and schools, all these and kindred subjects afford themes of thought and comment, and are naturally forced upon our attention, as we sit together for the first time in a new building to be devoted to their management. But your patience would weary, and my strength would fail, in the attempt to give them that elaborate consideration which their merits demand.

As has already been stated, the first city government of Boston was inaugurated in 1822, at Faneuil Hall. Some of the municipal offices remained in that ancient edifice a number of years; others were located in what was then called the County Court House, the building formerly on this spot, in which the meetings of the Common Council were held. On the two-hundredth anniversary of the settlement of the town, September 17, 1830, the old State House having been remodelled for the purpose, the different branches of the government, which had previously been in separate buildings, took possession of it, and an address was delivered by the Mayor, Harrison Gray Otis. On the same day appropriate commemorative services, of a popular character, took place at the Old South Church, an address being delivered by Josiah Quincy, the second Mayor of Boston, and a poem by Charles Sprague. The city government remained in the old State House about ten years, when another change took place, and it removed back to this spot, bringing with it other additional departments of the public service. The edifice was formally dedicated as a City Hall, March 18, 1841, by an address from Jonathan Chapman, then Mayor of the city. The corner-stone of the edifice in which we are now assembled was laid December 22, 1862, — the anniversary of the landing of the Pilgrims at Plymouth, — with appropriate Masonic services and an address by the Mayor, Joseph M. Wightman. This is the first building, therefore, which has been built and specially designed for municipal purposes; and the present government will have the satisfaction, before their term of office has expired, to see its administrative offices suitably established, with the best facilities for the accommodation of our citizens and the despatch of public business. We have no inspiring historical associations connected with this edifice, as had our predecessors, who occupied Faneuil Hall and the old State House; but the vicinity reminds us of the early past, as we look into the ancient burial-ground by our side, and recollect that Johnson and

Winthrop, the fathers of the town, have, for upwards of two centuries, been sleeping within its sacred enclosure; and that not far distant rest the bones of Hancock and Adams, and other patriots of another historical period. Nor can we forget that, on the very spot where the statue of Franklin is located before our windows, he played as a Boston schoolboy; and that within a stone's throw still stands the Old South Church, so redolent with the patriotic memories of other days.

We, and our successors in office, are to give this new building a name and character. May its symmetry and beautiful proportions be emblematical of the purity of life and elevated principles of those who shall occupy these seats, fill the several departments of public service, and manage the municipal affairs of this city! The past is secure. The general character of our government from the first has been a fitting representative of the reputation of our people. Few names upon our Municipal Register we could wish blotted from the roll; for no city has been more favored with faithful and devoted public servants. The most affluent in fortune, the highest in social position and culture, have deemed it an honor to participate in the conduct of our civic affairs, and citizens who had distinguished themselves in some of the most exalted national positions, have put on again the badge of office, and devoted their time and talents for the promotion of the city's welfare. We have seen in other large municipalities, paradoxical as it may appear, that those citizens who have the most at stake, and whose fortunes and happiness are dependent in a great measure upon good government, are the very ones who take the least interest in their local affairs, and those who would have exerted the best influence, on account of their intellectual gifts or moral character, shrink, as from pollution, from the discharge of those duties which they cannot neglect without detriment to the public weal. A municipality is formed to organize order, to afford protection to persons and property, and to secure the blessings of peace and prosperity to a community. These can only be accomplished by the active and zealous interest of the best men. They should occasionally take office themselves, when their services are needed; and they should always watch with a jealous care the tendencies of public measures and the motives of those who originate them. If Boston has acquired any reputation in the conduct of her internal affairs, it is because her people have so distinguished themselves in these matters; and when it shall be otherwise, her glory will have departed, and she should give up the right of self-government, for she will no longer deserve the privilege. The pride which a Bostonian feels in his city, whether he was born within its limits or has made it his home by adoption, is justified by its past history, its actual condition, and its future prospects. Our business men are not, as in some other localities, mere seekers of fortune, temporary sojourners until that object is accomplished, but they are a part of the living community, identified with all its concerns, and looking forward to spending the evening of their days within its precincts, or within the influence of its cherished associations. Hence a public spirit is fostered, which pervades every class and condition, which interests itself in every cause which will add to the good name and fame of the city, and which in the affluent is so often illustrated in the liberal endowments of our literary and charitable institutions.

In ancient times cities were established, under a different form of civilization, for mutual protection of the people, and were surrounded with walls and fortifications as a defence against a common enemy. Now, business is their mother, and while it is the chief interest and the greatest element in their outward growth, they become the great centres of mischief unless there is in the inhabitants a love of religion and virtue, and a taste for those objects of nature and art which ennoble the mind and refine the character. I do not believe, with Jefferson, that "great cities are great sores," for I hold that municipalities were the first to be identified with the cause of popular liberty; but we may accept the remark as a warning, and endeavor to make our city the great fountain from which shall spread those influences which shall be for the healing of the nation.

In addition to the local associations connected with this day, it is well to remember that it is also the anniversary of the adoption of the Constitution of the United States. Sharing with the whole country in the blessings of the Union, no city has been more loyal than Boston, or has exhibited better proofs of its devotion to the National Government. The late infamous attempt to destroy the integrity of the Republic at once aroused her patriotism, and she proved, through the long and protracted struggle, that the fires of liberty, kindled by the fathers, were still burning on her altars. Her sons went forth to the field of battle, or stood upon the decks of our naval ships, taking their lives in their hands for the common defence, while her daughters lent their ministering aid by the bedsides of the wounded and dying in the hospitals, or, remaining at home, comforted and cheered the absent by their timely contributions to their pressing needs. The old flag, whose beautiful colors have always mingled gracefully with the atmosphere which surrounds our habitations, now floats over a reunited country. Streaming in the free air as the representative of noble ideas and a great nationality, the best interests of humanity fostered and protected under its ample folds, its honor an absorbing passion, the people of Boston will be the last to submit to its humiliation, and with a resolute spirit will defend its fair fame, whether assailed by domestic traitors or foreign foes.

To-day, then, gentlemen of the City Council, on this double anniversary, with the associations connected with the memory of the ancestors who laid the foundations of this city, and the statesmen who framed the Federal compact which gave constitutional life to a nation, we appropriately dedicate an edifice for the home of municipal legislation. Its deliberative halls may never echo with the sublime eloquence which stirs the hearts of the people in senatorial chambers, or inflames their passions in the popular assemblies; the subjects of discussion may be prosaic, but their results will affect the happiness and comfort of many homes. We would dedicate these walls to the cause of good order and good government; to a watchful care of the morals of the community; to a zealous stewardship of all its public interests! Let the narrow spirit of party and partisanship stop at the threshold and seek other theatres for the display of their intrigues! Let official power be considered a sacred trust to be exercised by the most worthy citizens,— the possessor himself the bright exemplar and representative of the highest standard of public virtue! Let wholesome laws and wise ordinances advance the material prosperity of our beloved city, and the personal welfare of all its inhabitants! And with a filial obedience to the commands of the Great Ruler of the Universe, in whose hands are the destinies of communities as well as individuals, may the prayer of the people be ever that on the city seal: —

"*Sicut patribus sit Deus nobis.*"

As God was with our Fathers, so may He be with us.

www.ingramcontent.com/pod-product-compliance
Lightning Source LLC
LaVergne TN
LVHW011122110826
845150LV00008B/2228
* 9 7 8 1 4 1 8 1 9 5 4 4 1 *